All Along Life's Journey

To Charles & Teresa,
God bless you
in all that you do.
Love,
Claudia Stewart
12-17-96

All Along Life's Journey

Claudia Dianne Stuart

A Lyceum Book
Carlton Press Corp.
New York

Manufactured in Canada
ISBN 0-8062-5404-1

It gives me great pleasure as a writer and artist to be able to share my work with so many. The inspiration I get comes from those who touch my life in many ways and at various times. I feel so very blessed to have two beautiful grandchildren bringing joy into my life each day. For that, I dedicate this book of poetry to Raquelle Dianne Lawrence and Christian David Shorten. I can only hope and pray that the things I do help in some way to make this world a better place for them.

Claudia Dianne Stuart

Contents

Foreword

Once again Claudia Dianne Stuart is letting us into her world. She invites us to travel with her as she shares poetry that takes us *All Along Life's Journey*—her life, her journey. However, you will see that her journey might also be yours or mine. Reading this book allows the reader to behold Ms. Stuart's true essence. You will see that the author is motivated and inspired by her inner self, family, friends, community, and world. On the other hand, her writings have the ability to motivate and inspire others. You will relate psychologically and emotionally to her poetry. You may even find yourself thinking about and pondering your own life journey.

As you experience "Travel II" and other places far beyond with the author, you may think she has her head in the clouds. However, she jolts you back to reality with such timely poems as "Holocaust" and "Hands in the Air." This contrasting writing style shows what immense mastery Ms. Stuart has over her own feelings and emotions toward her environment. The ability to verbalize and write in the form of poetry requires special talent. The author is willing to challenge herself and others in ways that are both moving and entertaining.

Claudia Stuart is a noted professional, loving wife and gracious mother—my mother. I have had the pleasure of reading all of my mother's poetry that she had shared, published and unpublished. As usual, this book continues her tradition of beautiful writings. My mother is deeply rooted in her spirituality and family, which is evident in various selections. We are able to share her innermost thoughts and encounter the sheer emotion that comes through her poetry. Her present offering will not disappoint those who have read her previous publications. For those of you reading my mother's work for the first time, you are in for a unique experience.

Dietra L. Shorten

All Along Life's Journey

I

Special Ones Along the Way

My Lord

I can hear you
Singing through the trees
Rustling the leaves
Mounting the waves
In the stillness of caves.
I can see you
Blowing the wind
Believing it can
Remove all sin
Even deep within.
I can taste you
As honey from the bee
Salt from the sea
Fruits of the seed
And bitters of the weed.
I can feel you
Surrounding me with love
Giving a great big hug
Sending up the dove
And our hearts a tug.

Mother

You brought me into the world.
        Such love and understanding
Such warmth, care and concern.
And as I grew
        I knew
You were the special person in
My life.
You fed me
You changed me
You cuddled and cared for me.

I grew up strong
I grew up with a lot of love
I felt the love all around me.
You let me be myself.

You encouraged me to
        Reach for the stars
You supported my efforts
I felt successful.

At home
        In school
        At church
In life—I felt I could
        Achieve

I felt I could win
I felt I could love
You . . . I love you, Mother.

Daughters

I must take care of
my daughters

For I brought them into
the world to live, grow
and be happy.

Since birth they have
been such very special
people to me and I
feel honored just to be called
. . . Mom.

The very day I brought
them home, set up
a protection ring seldom
penetrated by the
other parent or relative
or friend or foe.

Through school, almost
the same—the ring—
the thing which teachers
always knew—whom—to
call, whom—to tell, and
whom—to see.

Traditions, rituals, and
occasions were great
opportunities for fun,
food and laughter.

How I love my girls
and it matters not
that one is grown and
gone and the other
is still at home.

For if I had my way
If I truly had my
way—I'd have
my girls with me always.

To protect, love and
to cherish . . . always.

A Woman Steady As You Go

A woman strong
A woman bold
A woman steady as you go.

A devoted wife
A caring mom
A woman steady as you go.

So full of love
A Christian, too
A woman steady as you go.

A friend to all
A teacher, too
A woman steady as you go.

A concerned heart
A helping hand
A woman steady as you go.

A voice that sings
The joy it brings
A woman steady as you go.

A dear, sweet soul
A child of God
A woman steady as you go.

You Are the One for Me

You are the one for me
That I can see.
Holding you near
That's where I'll be.

You are the one
That got away.
You are the one
For me.

You came to hold me
And keep me near.
You even called me
Honey, dear.

You, I can cherish
From time to time.
You are the one
For me.

You held me and loved me
Tried and true.
You are for me and
I'm for you.

You can forever
And ever say
You are the one
For me.

You came into my life
One stormy day,
Stole my heart and
Took me away.

You know that I
Will forever be
Close by your side
Just wait and see

You love me dearly,
I love you, too.
I will forever
Remember you.

You are for me and
I'm for you.
You are the one
For me.

Treasures

Life is made of so
many treasures—
family, children, parents
and goods and
services, too.

Honor thy father and
mother that thou
days may be long
upon the earth.

Keep the treasures near
to you and appreciate
more the significance
they have for you.

Never want that of
others because what
you have is also special
and unique in that
it belongs to you.

Sister

How I love you, sister
The words will easily flow.

I named you at your birth
And even watched you grow.

How sweet you were, so little
So cute and so carefree.

To thrive within the family
To be all that you could be.

I'm as proud of you today
As I was way back then.

To see your face all light up
And your dimpled grin.

Even when you're far away
We talk from time to time.

We share our assorted past
Oh, what's yours and mine.

The strength you have inside you
Will keep you safe from harm.

If you need me, just call me,
Share big sister's arm.

We Came from Yonder Shore

We came by water from
yonder shore
To see our homeland
nevermore.
We traversed the seas
through wind and rain
To roam the hills
never again.

We supped and sapped
yelped and yapped
Filled each galley way.
We were crimped and cracked
slapped and whacked
Through the night, till day.

Why take us from our
motherland
To bring us round the world?
Mandinka warriors and
Zulu prince,
Men, women, boys and girls.

And once here much work to
do
Let each man buy his slave.

Check his hair, teeth and arms
Strong, mighty from the grave.

Hard work is trifling upon the
land
Farming, picking and the like.
We look to the Lord for all our
help
As days wash into night.

That time is gone and we've
moved on
Now the 21st century.
We still work hard, and some
get paid
Believing we're yet free.

But look at all the welfare
rolls
Keeping mothers and children down.
Like nooses around from master's
hand
Their lives, their world are bound.

And even super athletes
Jumping, jogging and such.
We watch TV and feel awfully
proud
They please us very much.

But what happens when the cameras
stop
And no more pay TV?
What happens when the white man
says
Those cameras are just for me?
Gone are the endorsements for
Michael Jordan types.
Gone are the season's specials
Reserved now for whites.

We must look within for what we
do
To sustain us for all time.
Start out small to gain success
Building on the dime.

The pride will be uncovered
The faith will be revealed.
The love for one another
Will conquer the ill will.

The mighty who are among us
Will surface to take the lead.
The men so strong and healthy
Will plant wind ripened seed.
The joy is in the season
A new history to unfold.
The streets are straight and narrow
Paved end to end with gold.

The children are oh, so happy
The parents are there, too.
Granddaddy, aunts and uncles
Grandmamma, cousins, too.

We'll build a new tomorrow
Because we've learned from the past.
That only if it's ours
Will make our nation last.

God truly is our Master.
We owe Him all the pain,
The joy and our salvation,
He makes us great, again.

Epic Poem

Five years old and growing
Inch by inch each day.
Learning new things and knowing
How fun it is to play.

To be an adolescent
And running by the mile
Keeps fun within the realm
And laughter with a smile.

At ten years old the decade past
Never to see again.
Clinging close to family
Being the next of kin.

Now come the dreaded preteen years
With wanting to be big.
Squelching all the youthful fears
Feeling such a pig.

As teenagers we feel grown-up
Having hurried through our past.
Bring on the cars and movie shows
It's my life at last.

College is a useful tool
Preparing us each day
To make the bucks to lead us on
Throughout the Milky Way.

Off go our hats to victory
With diploma in our hand.
We knock on doors of employment dreams
Leaving out contraband.

Beware of those so intent
On building lives of dreams.
Dating, courting, being about
Isn't all it seems.

Searching high and low for one
To live with through the years
Can be precisely what you want
To show that someone cares.

With kids in tow and career intact
One travels the roads of life.
Keeping in mind bad times and good
The joys and sometimes the strife.

There can be so much harmony
That comes with great success.
Knowing that with the help of God
You won and did you best.

Now as you look back over your life
Just this one so short-lived.
Be ever thankful and grateful, too
And never just so glib.

For on and on your path shall go
Through ages past and new.
Travelling through ancient times ago
Living lives—a few.

With God as the spirit
Leading you to a cause,
Gives you ample time to reflect
Realizing your journey is but a pause.

Jump Jump

Jump Jump, my brother
from Africa
Jump Jump, without delay.
Don't you want to be really
free?
Go ahead and jump today.

Today is not mine to
jump
I am yet strong and proud.
To Gambians and Mandinkas
Jumping is not allowed.

Jump Jump, you slave upon
the ground.
Why don't you jump today?
The chains of steel upon your
legs
Prevent your running away.

I will not jump though I am
fit
To take my life away.
I'll make it through the test
of time
And watch my children play.

Jump Jump, in time of
freedom
Jump Jump, there in the bay.
Will I be the one to push
you in
And watch you float away?

I will not jump for the rebel
cause
Kill off my mother's hand.
The pen has inked the pact today
We have laws upon this land.

Jump Jump, to drink water
freely
Jump Jump, to your final place.
There's no one here that's willing
To fight the black man's case.

I do not look to you,
boy
To tell me what to do.
Remember I'm the one who worked
To build this country, too.

Jump Jump, for we despise
you
Your singing, shouting and
such.

Why do you still laugh and
dance
And kick about so much?

Jump Jump, to us is sinful
And it takes without a doubt
The freedom to enter the Kingdom
And walk around heaven throughout.

Jump Jump, for you are
foolish
Go ahead and jump today.
Who says your Christ is
watching
Who cares about your deeds today?

My Christ is all our Father
We are the image of Him.
Jump Jump—I'll jump for Glory
And all the joy within.

I'll jump because I'm happy
And land upon the ground.
Why don't you jump among
us?
All this jumping around.

Jump Jump, into the circle
Jump Jump, without delay.
The ring of life is turning
Let's see it shine this day.

Jump Jump, into the sunset
Off on yonder shore.
Jump with hands in the air
Singing evermore.

Jump Jump, bring your
brother
And all the kin between.
This is how it was written,
This is how it was seen.

We Came

We came from mighty kings and queens
Across the ocean blue.
My Great-grandfather was a mighty man
Grandfather and Daddy, too.

We came on ships
To the barren land
Enslaved one and all.
We worked our fingers
To the bone
And had to heed to call.

We came from strong, strong women
Ones from hearty stock,
Who travelled far and had it hard
But would rise to meet the mark.

We came from kings and queens abroad
Such pride within our loins.
A country bright and beautiful
With many jewels and coins.
We are a proud, proud regal folk
So mighty with the sword.
Believing in self and justice, too
And great faith in our Lord.

Holocaust

The ruins
            the human destruction
The annihilation of an
            entire race of people.

Who can care?
            Who can know the
            torment and
            utter devastation?

Who can defend these
            merciless acts?

Challenge us all never
            to forget
Never to allow and
            never to condone or concede.

Wipe the tears for you
            must see clearly.

Focus on the acts and
            never forget.

The Eyes

Look into the eyes and
see the sorrow
The despair, the hopelessness.

Look into the eyes and
see the mirrored soul.

The innocence
The longing to know
what is to come.

The trusting souls marching
to death and destruction.

Look into the eyes of
the children
Those young lives lost
forever in a sea
of annihilation.

Look into the eyes to
see the reflection of
your heart; never to see this
again.

Wake Up, My Soul

Wake up, my soul for
I hear new voices
new people longing
to be free.

Wake up, my heart to
reach out to others
who are silent
yet hurt, much.

Wake up, my mind for
new ideas and ways
to console others in
their time of need.

Wake up—wake up—wake up
If you sleep now
who will be there
to hear, to feel and
to act?

Wake up, my soul
for the souls
of others
are waiting.

Nothing in Common

Nothing in common
With you anymore.
It's over, I'm finished
I'll walk out the door.

When you say you love
me
I don't feel the same.
Don't worry sweet baby
You're not only to blame.

I've changed through the
years
That you were away.
And now that you're
back
I have this to say:

Nothing in common
With you anymore.
It's over, I'm finished
I'll walk out the door.

The love that we shared
Through thick and through thin

Was one in a million
I won't have again.
For you were my first
love
It pleased me so.
But I'm grown now
It's over
Just let me go.

Nothing in common
With you anymore.
It's over, I'm finished
I'll walk out the door.

A Class of People

I know all the
1%'s.
Those who do not fit
into any chart or form
To find their meager
niche.

I know all the
1%'s.
When added can
amass
A town, a country, a
nation, too.
Now, let's
consider class.

Our Wedding Day

It's our wedding day.
So wonderful
Such glee.

I have found the one I love.
You found love
in me.

We have so much
to look forward to.
We have come a ways
thus far.

I will be here for you.
You are now
my star.

We walk arm in arm
together
With love and hope
to share.

We have each other
to cherish
Because we said
we care.

Before the eyes of God
We commit to each
other now.

We hold these truths
as evidence.
We take our solemn
vow.

To love throughout eternity
Through sunshine and
through rain.

Through the joys of life
before us
Through sickness and
through pain.

Our love is never-ending
We share each
others' bliss.

We leave as one
on this day
Sealing it with a kiss.

I Wish You Were Here

A thousand miles away
    When I think of you
Seeing you, kissing you
    Wanting you
Holding you, needing you
    Loving you
I open my eyes and
    You are gone.

Out of here, away from me
    Leaving me
Life goes on and
    We must be strong
But whispering each
    And every day
I wish you were here . . . .

Friendship

How I long for special friendships
	Sharing time and point of view.
Being there for one another
	Recalling dreams anew.

How I want a special magic
	Uncommon to say the least.
To feel, to touch, to be aware
	Of emotions to unleash.

How I long for lively debate
	Over issues one or two.
To challenge the spirit and forge ahead
	Seeking for what I can do.

How I cherish that understanding
	That comes through listening
And honoring and respecting
	And most of all caring.

How I long for special friendships
	Sharing time and point of view.
I truly want to be a friend
	And find the same in you.

Missing You

I miss your heartbeat
    Next to mine.
All the stories that
    We shared.

I miss your smile
    And comfort
And the feeling that
    You cared.

I miss the walks
    Along the beach,
Water rushing along
    The shore.

I miss the tiny
    Little treasures
You once considered
    Yours.

I miss the rides
    In the country,
Farm animals along
    The way.
The bulls, goats

And sheep,
With dogs keeping
Them at bay.

I miss the
Little taverns
And the tables
All outside,
Opening the world
Around us,
The sky so high
And wide.

I miss the closeness
Of your touch
And the twinkle
In your eye.
Knowing our time
Would end
And we'd have to
Say good-bye.

But I wish you all
The happiness
That your world
Can endure.
And the love for
You—my darling
Is lasting, lasting
Evermore.

Forget Me Not

Forget me not,
Said from time
To time,

Reminds us of
A chance
Sublime.

And here to
Tell
Again one day

Of special
Words we
All must say.

I am here
For you
Till death do us part.

I keep you
Near
Within my heart.

Second Chance

I watch you
        Still in my dreams
Floating in and out.

The body strong
        Lean and mean,
That's what you're about.

Flights of fancy
        Take me away
Savoring for the night

All the hopes
        Dreams and desires
Wrapped so very tight.

One reaches out
        To clutch so close,
Tearing at the chance

For one more cause,
        To be involved
In the throngs of hot romance.

Stubborn

I cannot be what
You want me to be

I've got to be myself.

The pride is there
Inside of me.

I can't be someone else.

You couldn't shake yourself
And say

I'll change to meet demands.

Life cannot fit
Your wishes to

Change me for your own plans.

To be is
So important

Even this day and time.

You keep for you
That which is yours

And, by God, I'll keep what's mine.

Soft Is the Heart of a Child

Soft is the heart of a child
Crying out to be helped, held and heard.

Soft is the heart of a child,
A human being on the face of the earth.

II

Journey to Places Far Beyond

Travel I

Time travel across the ages,
    Visiting meccas and Sphinx.
Seeing the people of many lands,
    Conditions same and different.

Vistas of an ancient time,
    Columns long ago built.
Terrain so massive and forests few,
    Waterways dotting the land.

Speaking in many tongues,
    Longing to be heard.
Colorful majesty oft abounds,
    Folklore, folk tales and folkway.

Go On

The time has come
To make a move
No matter if you
Cannot choose.

Go on despite,
Without delay.
It is bound
To be okay.

Look to the hills
For all your help
And the result
Will aid yourself.

Many things are
Tried and true,
But happiness
Depends on you.

Vast Blue Yonder

Way across the vast
Blue yonder,
There on fleeting shore

Stands the tree on
Which to ponder
And the ocean
Nevermore.

Life is all but one
Big island
Filled with love
And hope.

Creating awe and lots
Of wonder,
Many ways to cope.

All the fear has
Yet subsided
Leaving pain at bay.

How the tempest seems
To squander,
Wiping sad times
Away.

Look to the sky with
        Birds a'many
Fluttering all about.

Call upon your own
        Strength and senses,
And mainly on your
        Clout.

Take the risk to
        Make the changes
All while life is
        Here.

The best times are yet
        Upon us,
Nothing, nothing more
        To fear.

Travel II

Flying high
Above the sea
Above the surf
And sand.

Seeing what there
Is to see
All across
The land.

Travelling through
The maze of time
Trimming here
And there.

Searching for adventure
Countries here
And everywhere—
Places where you dare.

Snowbirds

Snowbirds,
Snowbirds,
Flying south
Only to keep warm.

Flying high
Up in the clouds
Safely from
All harm.

Wings duck in and
Wings duck out
For the food
Below.

Making circles
In the sky
However fast
They go.

The Trip

I saw your eyes
        Before I left
Such pain and
        Tenderness.

I walked out and closed
        the door
Leaving our little
        Nest.

We traveled to the airport
        and we kissed
And said
        good-bye.

The tears welled up in
        our eyes
Both struggling not
        to cry.

So now the plane
        takes off
And enters the space
        of clouds.

And I think of all
    the things we said
And often, right
    out loud.

So now the time
    ticks by—and
I'll see you once
    again.

When I come home
    tomorrow
You'll wonder
    where I've been.

Little Bird

Fly away little bird
High in the sky
Soaring to great height.

The wind, the rain
The sunshine, too,
Go on with all your might.

When you finally
See below
Something you might like,

Go after it with
Zeal to kill and
Begin again your life.

Surviving

Good-bye always seems
        So far away
When departing in a car.

Facing the steering
        Wheel device and
Across your heart a scar.

The memories of the
        Past come clear
As in the mirror shines:

It's over and done,
        The motor runs
Perhaps, for brighter times.

III

Visions of a Brighter Day

The Vision

I have a vision of people
Many people—
Jews, Christians,
Buddhists, Baptists,
Muslims, Methodists,
Blacks, Whites,
All ethnic groups,
Men and women,
Children, too—

All marching up the
Side of the mountain
Reaching the top—together,
Crossing to the other side
Down into the rich, rich
Valley below.

The bountiful fields
The harvest of plenty
Enough for everyone
The more that come
The more there is.
People helping each other
To what they need
Food, water, shelter,
Love.

Nothing—nothing here to die for.
Nothing—nothing here to fight for.
Nothing here to laud over—
Everyone has the same.

All provided
All generously given
All graciously atoned for
And all miraculously
Keep sprouting forth
All from God, Almighty.
Thank you, Jesus
Thank you. . . .

Fantasy I

It's okay for you
To be
My fantasy
Today

As I hook onto
Wings so light
And start to
Fly away.

To listen to all the
Hopes and dreams
And remember joy
Afar.

To travel on roads of
Ecstasy
Unreachable by a
Car.

To heights above the
Crowds below
To pleasure centers
There.

And oh, the feelings
Quite remote
Knowing how much
You care.

I drop my head and
        Arms alike
To be picked up and be
        Driven.

And fall back upon
        My knees
Accepting the love I'm
        Given.

We twirl around in
        Broad daylight
Lasting into the
        Night.

The candles on and
        Burning low
Giving off enough
        Light.

To see the calm and
        Ebb and flow
Of our meeting special
        Needs.

The oil, the sweat,
        The bittersweet,
The dripping of tiny
        Beads.

The feelings are so
        Beautiful,
The caring and sharing
        And just

To keep the love
Alive
Between us is a
Must.

But now you're gone and I'm
Alone
With memories of the
Past.

Even through the years
Together
We knew it couldn't
Last.

Life goes on and we move
On
Living worlds
Apart.

Yet all the love and times
We've shared
Are indelible upon my
Heart.

All I do is close my
Eyes
And slowly drift
Away.

The swirl of thoughts is
Coming now,
You're here with me
Today.

I'm Loving You Too Much [A Song]

I'm loving you too much
I'm loving you too much
I'm loving you too much
        And this I know.

But even though
        I know it's so
I cannot let you go.

I'm loving you too much
        This I know.

I'm needing you so much
I'm needing you so much
I'm needing you so much
        And this I know.

But even though
        I know it's so
I cannot let you go.

I'm needing you too much
        This I know.

I'm wanting you too much
I'm wanting you too much

I'm wanting you too much
And this I know.

But even though
I know it's so
I cannot let you go.

I'm wanting you too much
This I know.

I'm loving you too much
I'm loving you too much
I'm loving you too much
And this I know.

But even though
I know it's so
I cannot let you go.
I'm loving you too much
This I know.

Attitude

Always look on the
Bright side.

Flip the coin
It's shiny new.

See the sun on
The horizon.

Think what you
Have to do.

Stiffen the back
Of great resolve.

Meet obstacles
Head on.

Life is no longer
In a fog.

Now you can
Be strong.

The past is over
And done with.

A better day is
    Today.

Tomorrow will be
    Brighter still.

All troubles are
    Washed away.

Attitude makes
    The difference.

Make up your
    Mind to be

Whatever, however
    And whomever

You truly want
    To see.

Dressed in your
    Own clothes,

Walking that
    Signature gait,

Puts you at the front
    Of the line

While others
Have to wait.

But just as today
Is over

And the tasks
All complete,

Tomorrow will be
Some others' time

To challenge and
Compete.

But that's okay
Because it takes

All kinds to make life
Go round.

And you'll see
Chances, many more

Before being placed
In the ground.

Fantasy II

He comes to me in the dark of night,
Gathers me up real close.
Says he would like to take me now
Because he loves me the most.

I look into his big brown eyes
As he holds me so tight.
He kisses me on the neck and ear,
Caresses me through the night.

Why come only when I close my eyes,
Drifting into my dreams?
You are so real and so alive
With love and zest it seems.

I don't want the day to come,
Leaving sweet dreams at bay.
Bringing on duties and chores alike,
Washing my friend away.

Thank goodness for imagination,
Conjured thoughts trickling down.
The relationships are endless,
Lost loves soon are found.

Rebound

Love is on the rebound,
Make it better than before.

All the many problems
Are swept beneath the door.

Starting fresh with love anew
With hope up in the air,

Gives way to dreams and fantasy
And eliminates despair.

Hands in the Air

Hands in the air
    Up, up, up.

I don't see them
    Pop, pop, pop.

Silence fell from
    Side to side.

No place else
    For him to hide.

He did everything
    The cop did say.

Did you have to take
    His life today?

A child of God, a son,
    A brother.

Not just him,
    Think of the other.

What is happening
    In the world around?

Let justice prevail
    Hear the sound.

The clanking doors of
    The bowels of hell

Because another
    Black man fell.

Hands in the air,
    Up, up, up.

I don't see them.
    Pop, pop, pop.

Just Move

It is not unusual to ask questions of the world around us. It is not awkward to dream about the wonderful possibilities that surround us.

What is unusual is not caring and never wanting to know. Never feeling the need to live and pursuing opportunities to grow.

Life is full of challenges and doors open from day to day. We need to be prepared to take our rightful place and lead.

Lead like we have never led before. Lead like our forefathers and mothers who blazed the paths for us. Lead like there is no tomorrow and today must stand for something and be something.

People watch and take notes on what's happening. People talk and query others about what is going on. People hear the messages we give and the way in which they are given. They can distinguish between the two. They know what is genuine and fake and futile and possible. And, of course, we know.

We know what we are capable of doing and setting the record straight. We know how far to push open wide the gate.

We survive by adapting to each changing fork in the road. We survive by mutant responses that are uniquely apropos.

We have a culture of strength, justice and fortitude. Believing in ourselves with perseverance and a strong attitude.

We can do anything our hearts would desire. We must pay the price for benefits and setting standards higher.

Sitting still brings nothing and leaves useful lives untapped. But with movement comes the joy of meeting bad times with attack.

With spirits high and rancor low—it's steady as you go. Keep all gathered within, we must continue to live and grow.

There are many lives yet to come and embark upon our path. Our life was full and most complete—
now
. . . the aftermath.

The Game

Sportsmanship, togetherness
Always for the team.

The stakes are high,
The field is fierce,

Realizing the dream.

We set our sights together
Knowing each has a part.

We fight on until the
end,

Bolting at the start.

In the name of competition,
Challenge and the like,

Armed with skill and readiness,
Poised, eager for this fight.

The first strike is against us,
Took us quite off guard.

We seem to say unto ourselves,
This game's going to be hard.

But nevertheless we rise
To meet the next attack.

I loom out in front,
The others watch my back.

What greatness is before us
As we measure and defend?

The name of the game is winning,
We are victors in the end.

Hope I

I reach out into the night
Are you there for me?
I see pitch black darkness
Don't you care for me?

I feel through the space in time
Seeking destiny.
I put on my badge of courage
And grab my progeny.

The path of life looms forward
There from coast to coast.
Opportunity is also knocking
Giving me the host.

The day is clear before me.
The rainbow lifted, too,
It's up to me to make it,
Starting life anew.

Just Go

Go away from my
    doorstep,
Go on down by the
    streetlight.
I don't want you by
    my side—no more,
Cause you don't
    treat me right.

Feelings

Question the as yet unknown
    To gain knowledge and wisdom.

Trust feelings and intuition,
    Fuel the desire.

Go with the flow and
    Heart abide.

Let the inside out
    Ever deep inside.

Love I

Send love,
    Receive love.
Reap love,
    lend love.
Be love,
    Get love.
Yet love,
    But love.

Happenings

Everything happens for a
reason and one must
follow his heart.

Do what feels good and
sensible and practical
and right.

Not just because someone
else wants you to.

Be true to yourself and
make yourself happy
and meaningful and
responsible and comfortable.

Listen to the voices
within and trust
they are significant and
important and reasonable
and helpful.

Love II

I love to fill a need in me,
A lust, a desire,
    The greed in me.

To be with someone to show so near
All the joy,
    That's why I want him near.

Holding close and touching back,
Erupting in
    The love attack.

I love to fill a need in me,
Caring and sharing,
    What love is to be.

Myths of Prediction

We look to the future
and think what
must be.

The course and the
numbers paint the
picture to see.

Yet, if we look back
and the presence
akin,

We see a different
truth and where
to begin.

Start today to make
changes and a few
stories to write.

And the future will
change,
almost overnight.

Hope II

Happy are we
When we understand
The desire within our hearts.

To be as one
Under the sun
Caring and sharing the parts.

Happy are we
To reconcile
The feelings so deep within.

Knowing full well
Any problems we have
Only time can mend.

Happy are we
To put aside
The harshness of the past.

So our love can grow
Into something sweet,
Trusting it will last.

Thankful for the Harvest

Turkey and dressing
    Filling the plate,
Piled high and to
    The sky.

Hurry to dinner and
    Don't be late,
Or no sweet potato
    Pie.

But first we bow our
    Heads this day
To praise the Lord, now
    Let us pray.

Thank you, Lord, for the
    Sun and moon,
The sea, and the water
    In it.

Thank you for the birds
    That fly,
The earth and
    People within it.

Thank you for the
    Fields of corn,
The bounty
    Oh, so great.

Thank you for the
Wonderful food
Filling now
My plate.

Thank you for the
Wind and rain
Bringing moisture
To the ground.

And all the animals
You made so well
That chase and
Play around.

Thank you for
The children
With innocence
So sublime.

Man and woman,
Boy and girl,
Occupying space
And time.

Thank you for
The harvest
On this
Wonderful day.

We pray for those
Who gave,
And those with
None to give away.

We pray for peace
    And harmony
As over the land
    We roam.

We pray for good
    Health and love
In each and
    Every home.

Thank you in
    The name of
Father, Son and
    Holy Ghost.

We pray in
    The name of Jesus
He alone
    Our Host.

Amen